NATIONAL GEOGRAPHIC KiDS

DEN HANDBOOK

YOUR GUIDE TO DECORATING, DECKING OUT, AND DESIGNING THE ULTIMATE EPIC DEN

TRACEY WEST

NATIONAL GEOGRAPHIC
WASHINGTON, D.C.

TABLE OF CONTENTS

WELCOME TO

ANiMaL JaM

THE ONLINE GaME FOR
KIDS WHO LOVE ANIMALS!

GET READY TO EXPLORE A WILD WORLD
WHERE YOU GET TO BECOME YOUR FAVORITE ANIMAL ...

In this live, multiplayer, online playground, you'll travel to the world of Jamaa to play games, meet new buddies, throw parties, explore awesome lands, and so much more—all while learning incredible info about animals. It's a world that's fun, educational, and THE place to be for kids who love animals and the outdoors.

There's so much to discover in Animal Jam, and that's where handbooks such as this one come in. It's filled with facts and tips that will help make your experience even wilder. Within these pages, you'll find out about the different types of dens in Jamaa and how to customize them, uncover behind-the-scenes secrets, and learn how to take your gameplay to the next level. The answers are all here!

SO, JAMMERS: Grab your handbook, log in, and get ready to become the coolest creature in Animal Jam!

PLAY SAFE

ANIMAL JAM IS A SAFE ONLINE ENVIRONMENT. But whenever you use the Internet, there are rules you need to follow to keep yourself and others safe:

1 **Never** share your real name, age, phone number, or home and email addresses with anyone online. Only share information that your parents say is OK to share.

2 **Never ever** give anyone your password. Somebody might promise to give you something cool if you give them your password. Don't do it. It's a trick!

3 **Never** meet anyone in person who you met on the Internet. Sometimes people aren't honest about who they really are.

4 **Always** be kind to everyone. Be friendly to other players and help us keep Animal Jam a happy place.

PLAY WILD ON THE GO!

There's more than one way to visit Jamaa, which makes the fun almost endless! Animal Jam – Play Wild! is the supercool mobile version of the game that has tons of the fun of Animal Jam, plus a few unique surprises. Read on to discover awesome info about Play Wild.

EVERY ANIMAL NEEDS A DEN

THERE'S A LOT TO DO IN JAMAA! You can roam different lands as a wild wolf, hop from shop to shop as a bouncing bunny, or explore the oceans as a speedy shark, awesome octopus, or other super sea creature. You can chat with other Jammers, go on Adventures, and rack up Gems playing games. But when your amazing day of discovery is over, where do you go?

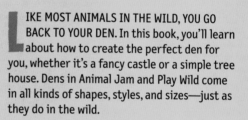

LIKE MOST ANIMALS IN THE WILD, YOU GO BACK TO YOUR DEN. In this book, you'll learn about how to create the perfect den for you, whether it's a fancy castle or a simple tree house. Dens in Animal Jam and Play Wild come in all kinds of shapes, styles, and sizes—just as they do in the wild.

You'll also get tips for decorating your den with the most incredible and astonishing den items. And because Animal Jam teamed up with National Geographic Kids to create the world of Jamaa, you'll learn some real-world facts along the way.

How do I get my den? you might be asking. *And how can I customize it to my style?* Your den adventure starts the very first time you log in ...

your FIRST DEN

AS SOON AS YOU VISIT THE WORLD OF JAMAA, YOU'LL GET YOUR OWN DEN. Every Jammer starts off with the same den, a cozy Small House.

FIND YOUR DEN: To get to your den, click the **Den button** on the bottom of your screen:

MOVE AROUND YOUR SMALL HOUSE AND EXPLORE. You'll find that it has a quaint one-story floor plan and a nice green lawn. After you explore, it's time to decorate your den.

Small House

INSIDER INFO

Before you start decorating your den, check out the dens of other Jammers. It's easy! Click another Jammer's name tag to see their Player Card, then click the **Visit Den button** 🏠. If their den is unlocked, you will be instantly transported there and be able to check out all the cool den items and decorations they have!

EDIT YOUR DEN: To start decorating your new home, click the **Edit Den button** at the bottom of your screen.

CLEAR DEN BUTTON: Click this to clear all items out of your den. (You'll find out how to add items on page 12.)

DEN LOCK BUTTON: Other Jammers can visit your den if you let them. Click the lock to control who can come hang out with you: Nobody, just your Buddies, or Everyone.

MUSIC BUTTON: You can change the music that you hear when you are in your den.

CHANGE YOUR MUSIC: Click the **Speaker icon** (🔊), then click the **Shop button** (🛒) to purchase new music for your den. Once you buy it, select it to play it in your den. You can change your music anytime by clicking the **Music icon** (🔊) and selecting what music you want to hear.

DECORATING BASICS

INSIDER INFO

Some items can only be purchased with Gems. If you only have Diamonds and Sapphires, you can exchange them for Gems at the Diamond Shop in Animal Jam, or the Sapphire Shop in Play Wild.

YOU CAN GET STARTED DECORATING YOUR DEN RIGHT AWAY. Every new Jammer is given a few den items when they start, but it's easy to shop for more.

1. Click the **Edit Den button** 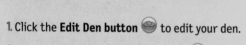 to edit your den.

2. Click the **Shop for Your Den button** .

3. Now you can see all the items available in Jam Mart Furniture. Use **Gems** to purchase items from this fun shop. When you exit the shop, you'll see your new items in your inventory at the bottom of your screen.

NOT SURE WHAT TO BUY FIRST? LOOK FOR ITEMS THAT CATCH YOUR EYE-ITEMS YOU'D LOVE TO HAVE IN YOUR OWN DEN AT HOME.

REMOVING AN ITEM: If you want to remove an item, hover over it with your mouse while you are editing your den. Then click the **X button**, and it will return to your inventory.

PLACING AN ITEM: Click an item, and it will appear in your den. Click and drag your mouse to move the item anywhere you want, and click the **orange arrow** to rotate it. When you close the inventory at the bottom of your screen, the item will remain where you left it.

Gems for your Den

ONCE YOU START DECORATING, YOU'LL WANT TO GET MORE STUFF. And to get more stuff, you'll need the three kinds of currencies used in Jamaa:

GEMS

DIAMONDS
(used in
Animal Jam)

SAPPHIRES
(used in
Play Wild)

There are a few ways to stock up on currency:

1. LOG IN: Members can earn Diamonds, Sapphires, and den items once a day when they log in.

2. PLAY GAMES: You can win Gems by playing tons of different games all around Jamaa.

3. USE CODES: Animal Jam codes can be found in magazines, advertisements, and official Animal Jam merchandise. AJHQ also releases special codes for holidays and other celebrations. Every code awards something different, from items and pets to Gems—and sometimes even Diamonds and Sapphires.

WINDOW:
Even though the Small House doesn't come with any windows, it's easy to add them.

Insider Info

You can buy new wallpaper and floors and change the look of your den with just one click. Here's a secret: In some dens, many of the wallpaper and floor styles will have unique patterns. The Rainbow Pink wallpaper, for example, looks like rainbow swirls in the Enchanted Hollow. In the Snow Fort, the rainbows look like they're covered with frost.

DENS: AN INSIDE LOOK

Feeling wild? Feeling artsy? Feeling sporty? Whatever your mood, there's a den for you! There are more than 30 dens to choose from in Animal Jam, and more new dens are being introduced all the time!

Making THE SWITCH

THERE ARE DOZENS OF DIFFERENT DENS TO CHOOSE FROM IN JAMAA! You can switch out your den for a new one at any time. Don't worry— you won't lose your old den when you switch. You can change from den to den, and your old den will be exactly the way you left it.

HERE'S HOW TO SWITCH YOUR DEN:

1. Go to your den and click the **Edit Den button** .

2. Click the **Switch Your Den button**.

3. Browse the options and choose the den that's right for you.

4. The new den will then be available in your **Switch Dens** menu.

5. Click the new den to make it your new home!

6. If you ever get tired of one of your dens, click the **Recycle Den button** in the Switch Dens menu and you can recycle it for Gems!

LAND AND SEA

In Animal Jam, you can play as either a land animal or an ocean animal. If you are an ocean animal, you can purchase an underwater den. If you switch dens to an underwater den, you will automatically go there as an ocean animal.

CHOOSING NEW DENS

NOT SURE WHICH DEN TO BUY? Here are some tips for choosing a den that will feel like home sweet home:

- *Pick one that you think would be the most fun to live in.* Eagles might be happiest on a tall peak; bunnies might prefer something underground.

- *Choose one that matches your interests. Do you love to curl up with a good book? A cozy cottage may be perfect for you. Or if you love travel and adventure, ancient ruins might be more your speed.*

- *Be sure to click the* **Preview button** *so you can explore a den before you buy it.*

INSIDER INFO

You can also buy dens in the Diamond Shop in Jamaa Township and the Den Shop in Coral Canyons. After you purchase a den, it will show up in your inventory when you click the **Switch Your Den button**.

> SOME DENS CAN BE FOUND BOTH IN ANIMAL JAM AND PLAY WILD. OTHERS CAN ONLY BE FOUND IN ANIMAL JAM, AND STILL OTHERS CAN BE FOUND ONLY IN PLAY WILD!

The Volcano can be found only in Animal Jam.

The Moonlight Manor can be found only in Play Wild!

PRINCESS CASTLE

This pretty castle is something straight out of a fairy tale. If you love stories about princesses living in palaces, then this castle is perfect for you. (It's also a great den if you're a fan of the color purple. This palace is purple inside and out!)

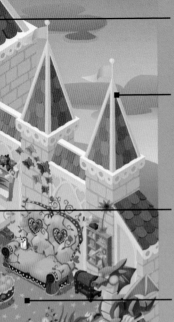

DARLING DETAILS

Heart-shaped details, pink bricks, and purple shingles make this one of the sweetest dens around.

TERRIFIC TURRETS

In medieval times, castles had towers such as these, called turrets, so guards could shoot arrows at approaching enemies. Turrets were later used for decoration.

A GRAND ENTRANCE

Make a dramatic entrance at this grand foyer. In medieval castles, spiral staircases generally spiraled clockwise (from the ascender's point of view), giving right-handed attackers a disadvantage.

PARTY TIME

A spacious first floor is great for hosting your buddies.

SWEET DREAMS

You might sleep soundly in this den, thanks to the sweet-smelling rose bushes that border the castle. According to one study, smelling pleasant scents, such as roses, when you sleep may give you happy dreams!

AJ Stats

GAME: Animal Jam and Play Wild
DEN TYPE: Land
COST: 6,000 Gems in Animal Jam; 150 Sapphires in Play Wild
SPECIAL WALLS AND FLOORS?: No
INSIDER INFO: The Pet Princess Castle is a tiny version of this den.
ONLY IN PLAY WILD: This castle sits in a beautiful forest on the shores of a peaceful lake.

CALIFORNIA'S CASTLE

Most people don't think of the United States when they think of castles, but one of the world's most famous ones is in California. In 1865, wealthy newspaper tycoon William Randolph Hearst bought land with the dream of building a huge estate. By 1947, the property, known as Enchanted Hill, contained a castle, gardens, pools, and the world's largest private zoo at the time. Many of the animals freely roamed the hills surrounding the castle. Visitors who drove up to the castle might have spotted deer, antelope, zebras, llamas, kangaroos, or big-horned sheep. Most of the animals were donated to other zoos by 1953, but some were left in the wild. The castle now belongs to the state of California, and descendants of those first zebras still roam the pastures around it.

Do you love the sun, the surf, and the sand? Do you dream of tropical islands when it's snowing outside? Then you'll love the Beach House—it's perfect for summer-loving Jammers! It's got fabulous views of the ocean and spaces that are perfect for hanging out with your buddies.

OCEAN VIEW
Enjoy the breeze and watch the seagulls soar from this open balcony.

SUN AND SAND
No matter what kind of Jammer you are, you can have fun at the beach! Even animals in the wild know how to make a splash: Penguins love Boulders Beach in Cape Town, South Africa, and adorable pigs have even taken over a beach in the Bahamas!

SOOTHING SOAK
Relax in the hot tub after a long day of swimming.

SLIP AND SLIDE
Slide into the water right from the deck. You won't find sharks in this Jamaa den, but if you zoom down the Leap of Faith waterslide in the Bahamas, you'll glide down a clear underwater tube through a shark-filled lagoon!

PORCH PARTY
A porch is a great place for an outdoor barbecue with your buddies!

A DUNE FOR A DEN

When you build a beach house, you've got to build it above the high-tide line, or it will just get washed away. Animals that live at the beach have the same issue. Any dens they build have to be protected from the ocean, wind, and predators.

On many beaches, the best place to do that is on a sand dune, or a hill of sand. A dune is usually created one grain at a time, as wind blows sand up on the beach. As the dune grows taller, plants take root, and the dune becomes larger and sturdier.

Some shorebirds, such as Wilson's plovers, build their nests in dunes. Plovers choose a spot next to a piece of driftwood or a clump of grass. The male birds scrape a few shallow holes in the sand, and the females pick the one they like best. Then the nests are lined with grass, pebbles, and pieces of seashell. The result? A beautiful bird beach house!

ENCHANTED HOLLOW

Do you keep your curtains closed in your bedroom? Do you feel most at home under the covers or in a blanket fort? Then an underground den might be just the thing for you! Nestled deep beneath the forest floor, this cozy den is perfect for getting away from it all.

SUNNY SPACE

You don't have to spend all your time underground in this den. This lawn is a great place for a garden or to throw a barbecue.

TERRIFIC TOADSTOOLS

You can find these mushrooms, which are a type of fungus, in some of this den's shady spots. Unlike plants, wild mushrooms don't need sunlight to grow.

COZY KITCHEN

There are lots of small rooms in this den that you can customize. Create a kitchen like this one, or an entertainment room, or a walk-in (or if you're a bunny: hop-in!) closet—it's up to you!

PERSONAL LIBRARY

This reading nook comes with a built-in bookshelf—but you can always fill it with more bookshelves from the shops.

COLORFUL CRYSTALS

The walls are embedded with beautiful, sparkling jewels. There are also real towns where gems might actually line people's walls! In the opal mining town of Coober Pedy, Australia, 80 percent of the population lives underground alongside the gems. That's because the outside temperature can reach 120°F (49°C) in the summer!

Wacky Warrens

Some rabbits make their home in underground tunnels called warrens. Their dens might not have wallpaper or books, but they're perfect for rabbits. Why?

Living underground helps keep rabbits safe from predators such as foxes, badgers, and weasels. Each warren has a few exit and entry holes, so rabbits can make quick escapes from predators when they need to.

Rabbit warrens are organized into separate spaces. There is a space for sleeping, a space for newborn babies, and even a space for rabbits to leave their waste—kind of like a bunny bathroom!

SPRING COTTAGE

No matter what season it is, you can always enjoy a breath of fresh air in your Spring Cottage. Start out in your roomy two-story cottage with a colorful straw roof, and then stroll through the multilevel forest clearing, complete with flowers and a bubbling brook.

FLORAL TOUCHES

This den has a rainbow of blooms! The scientific name for these blue-purple flowers, *Myosotis*, comes from the Greek term for "mouse's ear" and describes the shape of their petals. The English name is forget-me-not, which may be from a legend about a man who picked the flowers for his girlfriend before a river swept him away. His last words? "Forget me not!"

GAME: Animal Jam and Play Wild
DEN TYPE: Land
COST: 7 Diamonds in Animal Jam; 150 Sapphires in Play Wild
SPECIAL WALLS AND FLOORS?: Yes. Many of the styles get extra flowery when in the Spring Cottage.
INSIDER INFO: You can find all kinds of flowers and plants in the shops. Use them to turn the grounds of your Spring Cottage into a garden paradise!
ONLY IN PLAY WILD: In both games you get the same beautiful cottage and sprawling green grounds. But with tons of different items to choose in each game, the decorating possibilities are endless!

DECKED OUT
Chill out on your deck and gaze out at the pond.

NATURAL BEAUTY
This den even comes with a waterfall!

Great GardenS!

1

2

3

Let these gardens from around the world inspire you as you customize your own.

1. **Montreal Botanical Garden, Canada:** This amazing garden features larger-than-life sculptures made out of plants. You can make a sculpture garden with items from the Topiary Shop in Sarepia Forest.

2. **Keukenhof Gardens, Netherlands:** You'll find brightly colored flowers planted in rainbow patterns in this garden. Get the look by grouping flowers of the same color in your Spring Cottage. Accessorize with rainbow-themed den items.

3. **ACROS Fukuoka, Japan:** Designers added extra green space to the crowded city of Fukuoka by planting on the levels of the civic center. You can get a stepped look by loading your garden with den furniture of different heights and placing plants on top.

TiGer TeMPLe

Tigers live in rain forests, grasslands, and swamps. They also sometimes take shelter in old ruins and temples. That's why the Tiger Temple in Play Wild is a fitting home for these elusive felines. This beautiful stone den has lots of levels for a tiger to climb and explore.

TWISTING TREES

Nature and stone intertwine in this stunning den. At the Ta Prohm temple in Cambodia, trees like these have grown into the ruins, becoming part of them.

WATER FEATURES
Splash around in one of the many pools and waterfalls.

WILD PRINTS
Jaguar-print furniture adds a jungle touch to this den. The spots on wild jaguars are called rosettes.

STONE STATUES
These stone tigers really make a statement! Many ancient sites from around the world feature elaborate statues. The Bayon Temple ruins in Angkor Thom, Cambodia, feature more than 200 giant faces carved into 54 stone towers.

HAVE A BALL
Tigers are just big cats, after all. Add some toys for a playful touch.

THE RUINS OF RANTHAMBORE

Ranthambore National Park in India is 154 square miles (400 sq km) of jungle. It contains several bodies of water and is dotted with crumbling stone ruins. Once a hunting ground for royalty, Ranthambore is now a sanctuary for Bengal tigers. Twenty-two tigers live in the park, and they are all numbered and named. Their "queen," Machli, raised nine cubs of her own.

With plenty of deer to eat in the park, this protected land is perfect for wild tigers. Jeeps and trucks take sightseers through the jungle, where they observe the tigers playing, hunting, and climbing the ruins. Machli would even stay still while tourists took her photo!

A ROYAL SEAT
Some den items, such as this Tiger Temple Throne, go perfectly in this jungle den.

27

VOLCANO

Jammers who can take the heat will be right at home in this den. You can prowl the levels of a volcano glowing from within with red-hot magma. But don't worry—this Volcano won't be erupting anytime soon!

VOLCANIC VIEW

The top floor has a great view of a steaming volcano.

CANINE CARVINGS

Wolf sculptures are carved into the stone. There are several species of wild wolves, but scientists recently discovered a new species of wolf: the African golden wolf. They used to believe it was a type of jackal.

SCORCHED SYMBOLS

Who needs wallpaper when mysterious glowing symbols decorate your walls?

NATURAL LIGHTING

When it's below ground, liquid, melted rock is called magma. When it escapes through a vent in the volcano, it's called lava. In your den, the soft glow of magma sets an eerie mood.

AJ Stats

GAME: Animal Jam
DEN TYPE: Land
COST: 3,000 Gems
SPECIAL WALLS AND FLOORS?: No
INSIDER INFO: Low on Gems? This is one of the least expensive dens in Jamaa.

ROBOTS Get It DONE

In Jamaa, you can freely explore the Volcano without breaking a sweat, but in the wild, it's a different story. Scientists have measured the temperature of lava at more than 2000°F (1093°C). Inside a volcano, the bubbling magma can get even hotter!

Even if there is no magma present, exploring the narrow crevices of a volcano can be a challenge. These crevices, or fissures, are places where lava flows from the volcano during an eruption. Scientists want to make a map of these fissures so they can learn more about why volcanoes erupt. So what do scientists do when they want to get a close-up look of the inside of a volcano? They bring in the robots!

In 2014, NASA tested VolcanoBot 1 at Kilauea volcano in Hawaii, U.S.A. The little bot had two wheels and was only 12 inches (31 cm) long. It plunged 82 feet (25 m) into a fissure, collecting data to help researchers put together a 3-D map.

VolcanoBot 1 was just the beginning of robotic volcano exploration. NASA has been testing more VolcanoBots—and there are even plans to send them into space, to explore volcanoes on the moon or other planets.

LUCKY CASTLE

This mystical castle sits atop a cliff overlooking the sea. Misty gray clouds gather in the blue sky behind it. They're a reminder that you need rain to make a beautiful rainbow. This castle only pops up around Lucky Day, but if you grab it when you see it, you'll be one fortunate Jammer!

HARMONIOUS HARP

This golden musical instrument is a perfect decoration for this den. Harps are one of the symbols of Ireland, appearing on coins and on the Irish coat of arms. Tales of Irish harp players date back 1,000 years.

AJ Stats

GAME: Animal Jam and Play Wild
DEN TYPE: Land
COST: 5 Diamonds in Animal Jam; 150 Sapphires in Play Wild
SPECIAL WALLS AND FLOORS?: Yes. Many of the patterns take on a Celtic theme.
INSIDER INFO: Head to the right side of the Lucky Castle and slide down the rainbow to a pot of gold!
ONLY IN PLAY WILD: The castle has a slightly larger platform at the top level, with more room for decorating. And make sure to use the two additional towers for even more decorating fun!

PATTERNED PATIO

This pattern is known as a Celtic knot—a design made of a series of interwoven knots with no start or end. Such knots first appeared in Ireland and Scotland about 1,600 years ago as decoration on manuscripts.

LUCKY GREENERY

Add some four-leaf clovers for extra luck!

TUB OF TREASURE

You can't buy anything with this gold, but it's still fun to dance around in it!

THE LEGEND OF THE BLARNEY STONE

Looking for a spot where you can land a little luck? Head to Blarney Castle, located just outside of Cork, Ireland. Built nearly 600 years ago, this stone structure has become one the most famous castles in the world because of a certain lucky legend. One of its stones, known as the Blarney Stone, is said to have a magical power: Anyone who kisses it will be granted the gift of eloquence—the ability to influence others through speech.

The stone is located in one of the battlements—tower walls with holes in them, originally built so castle guards could fire at attackers. Because there is an open space between the floor of the tower and the battlement, you have to grab two strong poles and lean backward to kiss the stone. All that may sound like a lot to go through for a legend, but millions of lips have touched the Blarney Stone in the last 200 years. Does that mean there are millions of smooth talkers out there? Probably not—but they've all got at least one great story to tell!

31

SNOW FORT

When winter arrives, cold-loving Jammers can make the Snow Fort their den of choice. Overlooking the mountains and surrounded by a frozen forest, this den can be a sporty winter hangout or a fancy ice palace, depending on how you decorate it.

EXPERIENCE THE ELEMENTS

It's very cold in the fort's highest tower— so cold that if you stand there, you'll turn a frosty blue for a short time!

FROSTY FOREST

This castle is nestled in an evergreen forest. In the wild, evergreen trees lose their leaves or needles a few at a time and they grow right back, so the trees stay green all winter. Trees that have no leaves in the winter are deciduous. They lose their leaves all at once during the fall, and the leaves don't grow back until spring.

AJ stats

GAME: Animal Jam
DEN TYPE: Land
COST: 5,000 Gems
SPECIAL WALLS AND FLOORS?: Yes. Every style becomes frosted with snow and ice or snowflake patterns.
INSIDER INFO: Look for the Snow Fort in the Den Shop in December or January, where it usually sticks around until spring.

WINTRY WALLS

The walls and floors of this dazzling den are made of snow and ice. The Icehotel in Sweden is a real hotel built every year from "snice"—a mixture of snow and ice. The freezing temperature inside the hotel hovers around 20°F (-7°C).

SNOWFLAKE DECOR

Warm up your floors with a snowflake-shaped throw rug. Did you know that in just one ounce (28 g) of snow there are about 10,000 snowflakes? That's a lot of flakes!

A COLD BUT COZY CAVE

When mother polar bears are expecting babies, they dig cozy snow caves for their newborn cubs. Before winter approaches, mother bears find a snowdrift or a large snowbank. They dig a chamber big enough to fit in. They also might dig one or two extra chambers for the cubs they're expecting. Finally, they climb inside and let falling snow block the entrance to the cave, but they make sure to leave a hole open so that air can get in.

Most wild polar bear cubs are born in December. Mother bears do not leave the cave until March or April, when the babies are strong enough to survive outside. During that whole time, mother bears don't eat or drink! Once out of the cave, they will stay with their cubs for another two and a half years, teaching them how to take care of themselves in the harsh Arctic environment.

Art Gallery

Jammers love to create original works of art called Masterpieces. (For more on making your own Masterpiece, go to page 72). This den was created to give artists the perfect space to display their artwork. Once you place your favorite Masterpieces on the walls, invite your buddies over to admire them.

IN THE SPOTLIGHT

Custom lighting will shine on 30 Masterpieces, but you can squeeze in more artwork than that if you get creative!

ZEN SPACE

A peaceful koi pond helps create a calming atmosphere. Koi fish originated in Japan, when farmers noticed that some carp (a type of fish) had unusual colors and patterns. They bred these unique fish to create the colorful koi species.

WORLD'S WEIRDEST ART MUSEUMS

1

2

3

COME RIGHT IN!
You don't need a security guard at the entrance to your Art Gallery, but other museums do. The biggest art heist in modern times happened at the Isabella Stewart Gardner Museum in Boston in 1990. Two men dressed as police officers walked off with paintings valued at $300 million!

What's wonderful to one person might be weird to another. What do you think? Are these art museums wonderful, weird, or wonderfully weird?

1. **Barney Smith's Toilet Seat Art Museum:** This San Antonio, Texas, U.S.A., garage contains more than 1,000 art creations using toilet seat lids. Barney's inspiration? Maybe all those years he spent as a master plumber.

2. **Corn Palace:** Half a million tourists each year travel to Mitchell, South Dakota, U.S.A., to admire murals made of—you guessed it—corn.

3. **Momofuku Ando Instant Ramen Museum:** Do some food packages look like works of art to you? Then you'll love this museum in Osaka, Japan, which displays 800 instant noodle packages from around the world.

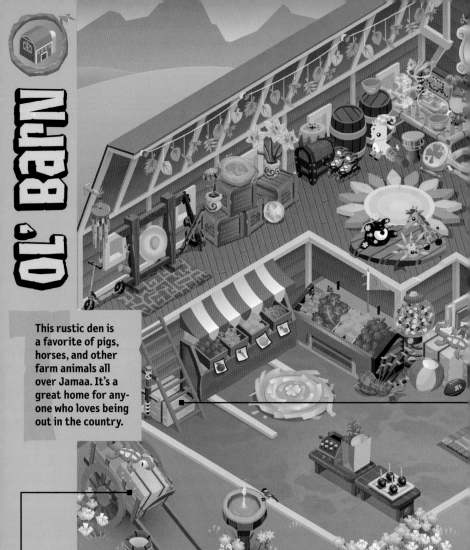

OL' BARN

This rustic den is a favorite of pigs, horses, and other farm animals all over Jamaa. It's a great home for anyone who loves being out in the country.

WHEELBARROW

What barn would be complete without a wheelbarrow? Historians think the wheelbarrow was invented in the rice paddies of China in about A.D. 200. Later, the Chinese military used the tool, which they called the "wooden ox" or "gliding horse," to transport supplies and wounded soldiers across the battlefield. Modern wheelbarrows are usually used for carrying light loads short distances—which makes them perfect tools for farmers.

GAME: Animal Jam
DEN TYPE: Land
COST: 5,000 Gems
SPECIAL WALLS AND FLOORS?: Yes. Look for horseshoes, hay, spurs, cowhide, sunflowers, or southwestern patterns.
INSIDER INFO: Thinking about inviting all your buddies over for a barn bash? Since the early 1840s, folks in the country have been throwing hoedowns, parties with lots of music and dancing. So make sure to turn up the music—try "Jam On" or "Train Trottin'"—and start dancing until your guests follow your lead.

HEY–IT'S HAY!

The barn is stacked with plenty of horses' favorite food. There's an old saying, "Make hay while the sun shines," that means the time to do something is when conditions are good. Rain can ruin hay, so farmers have to make sure to harvest theirs during dry, sunny weather.

WIDE OPEN SPACES

Run, leap, and play in the green grass surrounding the barn.

WHY DO PIGS LOVE MUD?

Do you have a messy bedroom? Then you may have heard an adult say, "Clean up that pigsty!" Pigs have a reputation for being dirty because they like to roll around in mud. But really, they're very clean animals. Yes, pigs do roll in mud, but they do it to keep cool on hot days. If pigs live in a cool barn or have a shady place to hang out, they stay very clean. So go ahead–mess up your den with as many items and accessories as you like. Just don't blame the pigs!

PEGASUS PALACE

While a barn may be the perfect den for a horse, a horse with wings needs something different. In Play Wild, Jammers can add Pegasus Wings to their horses and turn them into mythical creatures. And every Pegasus needs a house in the clouds!

TAKE FLIGHT

Wings keep this palace floating in the sky.

CUT THROUGH THE CAVERN

Enter the cave to reach the higher levels of the palace.

BEAUTIFUL BLUES

The walls and accents of this palace are all gorgeous shades of windy blue. When you decorate the inside of this den, try an all-blue theme with blue rugs, wallpaper, flowers, and more fun items.

NEED TO RELAX?

These winged items perfectly match this den's gorgeous crystal accents. Sit on your Pegasus Throne or Pegasus Couch and watch the gently flowing water in the Pegasus Fountain.

THE MYTH OF PEGASUS

You may know that Pegasus is a creature from Greek mythology. But did you know that this beautiful winged horse sprang from a hideous monster? Medusa was a monster with hissing, twisting snakes for hair. If she looked at you, you turned to stone. A hero named Perseus was sent to slay Medusa. He cut off her head, and Pegasus flew out of her neck.

Legend says after years of adventuring, the mythical horse became a constellation in the sky. If you live in the Northern Hemisphere, you can look for Pegasus among the stars from late summer into early fall.

Restaurant

This is the perfect den for Jammers who think cooking for friends is the best way to entertain. Get the thrill of running your own restaurant, and have fun decorating it any way you want. Do you want a fancy bistro? A Western-themed diner? A place that's perfect for tea parties? You can find den items for just about any theme in Jamaa's shops.

MAGNIFICENT MENU

A menu adds a tasty touch for this den. Menus have only been around since the late 1700s. Before then, people didn't go out to eat for fun. Taverns or restaurants served travelers on long journeys, and fed them whatever food the owner had on hand.

SCRUMPTIOUS SCONCES

The soft glow of sconces on the walls sets the mood for yummy food.

OPEN-AIR DINING

Set up some tables on the patio so your guests can dine in the fresh air.

AJ Stats

GAME: Animal Jam
DEN TYPE: Land
COST: 4,000 Gems
SPECIAL WALLS AND FLOORS?: No
INSIDER INFO: Keep your eye out for the Dinner Party, where Jammers come from all over to dine together in parties held in this den.

COOK'S PARADISE

Whip up your favorite treats in a state-of-the-art kitchen. Need some real-life inspiration? The most well-known kitchen in the world might be the one that the famous chef Julia Child used for her TV cooking shows. The whole kitchen is on display in the Smithsonian Institution in Washington, D.C.

DARING DINING

When do you need courage to order a hamburger? It might take bravery to eat in some of these restaurants in extreme locations around the world.

1. **Dinner in the Sky:** At this restaurant, diners are strapped into their chairs and are hoisted by a crane 160 feet (49 m) in the air. They eat their meal floating in the sky. The restaurant doesn't have a set location; it pops up in different cities around the world.

2. **Ithaa Undersea Restaurant:** This glass restaurant in the Maldives sits 16 feet (5 m) below sea level. Customers can dine while watching fish swim all around them.

3. **SnowRestaurant:** Every winter, a restaurant at SnowCastle, a resort in Finland, gets built out of ice and snow. Diners sit on ice chairs and eat their food off ice tables.

SKY KINGDOM

You don't have to be an eagle to live in the Sky Kingdom, but it helps if you're not afraid of heights! This den floats in the clouds high above Jamaa. It is made up of several small islands connected by pathways.

TOWERING TREES

A forest in the sky? Why not! In China's Zhangjiajie National Forest Park, trees grow on tall, rocky spires that rise into the clouds.

AJ Stats

GAME: Animal Jam
DEN TYPE: Land
COST: 7 Diamonds
SPECIAL WALLS AND FLOORS?: Yes, wallpaper only. Many of the styles take on the French fleur-de-lis pattern.
INSIDER INFO: So far, the Sky Kingdom holds the record for being the biggest den in Jamaa.

TAKE THE SHORTCUT

This rainbow slide connects to the large green slide—one of the longest slides in Jamaa. The longest nonwater slide in the world is London's ArcelorMittal Orbit, at 524 feet (160 m). Riders zip down the corkscrew slide at a top speed of 15 miles an hour (24 km/h).

RULE THE SKY

This three-story castle is one of the grandest in Jamaa.

SCULPTURE GARDEN

This crystal statue of Mira, one of the guardian spirits of Jamaa, sits at the center of the Sky Kingdom.

EAGLE AERIES

Bald eagles' nests, also called aeries, are an amazing example of avian architecture! First, the eagles choose a site high up in a strong tree, away from predators, and close to a water source. Next, they use large sticks to make the outside layer of the nest, which can be as much as 10 feet (3 m) wide. After that, softer materials such as dead weeds are used to line the nest. Finally, feathers, grass, and dry moss are added to cushion the area where the mother eagle will lay her eggs. Some nests have been discovered that weigh two tons (1.8 t)—about the same as two SUVs!

AQUARIUM

This incredible den allows Jammers to stock their home with all kinds of fish and sea creatures. The Aquarium doesn't come with any fish, but it does contain its own shop where Jammers can purchase sea animals to add to their den.

TAKE IT ALL IN
Glass floors and windows maximize your view of your sea creatures.

ENORMOUS AQUARIUM
At three levels high, the Aquarium is big enough and deep enough to hold large sea creatures, such as this orca. These whales can grow to 20 feet (6 m) long and weigh as much as six tons (5.4 t).

VIEWING PLATFORM
You can make your Aquarium guests comfortable with tables, chairs, and couches to sit on while they watch the fish.

INSIDER INFO

These special sea creatures aren't pets, and they can only be placed in your Aquarium. After you purchase your swimmers, you can put them in your Aquarium by tapping the **plus button** ⊕. (Not all fish can be placed in every slot.) When you're done, sit back and watch your new fishy friends explore their surroundings!

DON'T BE JELLY

You can fill your aquatic new den with all sorts of creatures, including jellies! Did you know that "jellyfish" aren't really fish? Because they have no backbones, they are classified as invertebrates. Many scientists use the term "jellies" to describe these sea creatures.

THE PROBLEM WITH PLASTIC

Some scientists think that by the year 2050, there will be more plastic objects than fish in the ocean! That's a real problem, and one that the Monterey Bay Aquarium in California, U.S.A., is working to fix.

The aquarium is tackling the problem in many different ways. They have an exhibit that educates visitors about plastic pollution, and they run a social media campaign about the problem. They're also reducing the use of plastic in their operations. And in 2016, they encouraged voters to pass a law in California banning single-use carryout plastic bags. Thanks to efforts like theirs, the ocean will be a healthier place for ocean creatures.

SUNKEN SHIP

Need a place to rest your flippers after a long afternoon of exploration beneath the waves? All aboard the Sunken Ship! Turn this wild wreck into a happy home that fits your swimming style.

PEEK THROUGH THE PORTHOLE

Portholes give you a window to the world outside your den.

SHIPWRECK AHOY!

It is estimated that there are approximately three million sunken ships in the world's oceans—and less than one percent of them have been explored.

INSIDER INFO

You can buy special underwater den items by clicking the **Shop for Your Den button** when you are editing your den.

AJ Stats

GAME: Animal Jam
DEN TYPE: Ocean
COST: 2,500 Gems
SPECIAL WALLS AND FLOORS?: No
INSIDER INFO: When you click the **Den button**, you'll go to the den you most recently played in, even if it's a land den. To play in your new ocean den, just click the **Switch Your Den button**, and soon you'll be swimming in your watery home!

SEA GARDEN

Who needs a lawn when you've got beautiful ocean life outside your door?

TREASURE TROVE

You can fill your sunken ship with all sorts of treasures. Some estimates say that there may be $60 billion in sunken treasure all over the world. Diving expeditions to find lost treasure can cost millions of dollars, and until that changes, most of it will remain in the ocean.

EXPLORING the Titanic

When you think of shipwrecks, one name probably comes to mind right away: R.M.S. *Titanic*. The sinking of this British luxury liner in 1912 has been the subject of books, movies, and even a Broadway musical.

For decades after the shipwreck, explorers tried to find the R.M.S. *Titanic*, with no luck. Then, in August 1985, scientist Robert Ballard decided to try. He had developed an underwater craft called Argo that had a remote-controlled camera. The Argo searched the floor of the North Atlantic at a depth of 13,000 feet (4,000 m). On September 1, Argo recorded images of the sunken *Titanic*.

This eventually led to the theory that while the *Titanic* did hit the iceberg, that collision might not be the only reason it sank. There was no evidence of a long gash in the ship's hull—just thin gashes and separated seams in the hull's plates that had let water flow in.

What does this mean? Some think that poor quality steel or rivets might have caused the hull to break and the ship to sink. One journalist speculates there might have been a fire that damaged the hull. For now, this mystery still needs more exploration.

MOONLIGHT MANOR

If you have ever dreamed of building the ultimate tree house, then Moonlight Manor is for you! There is always a full moon shining on this den, and it is an ideal home for nocturnal animals such as raccoons. But you don't have to be a masked mammal to enjoy this magical, multilevel den. It is filled with fun things to explore!

BLAST OFF

Climb out on one of the tree branches of this den and it will take you to a secret platform with a wooden rocket ship. Hop aboard to see what happens!

UNDER THE STARS

Climb the stairs to this platform to get a great view of the night sky. Keep your eyes peeled and make a wish when you see a shooting star!

WATER WHEEL

A water wheel adds charm to this den. Water wheels were likely invented more than 2,000 years ago. Throughout history, they were used for many things including irrigation, crushing grain, and powering iron forges.

NATURAL GLOW

Could there be fireflies glowing in these lanterns? Fireflies are a species of beetle that are bioluminescent, which means they can make their own light.

TREE HOUSE DECOR

Want a rustic feel to this den getaway? Light up the night with this Log Lamp, and put Log Benches indoors and out to complete the look.

COUNTRY DENS, CITY DENS

If you were a raccoon, would you rather live in the country or the city?

If you lived in the country, you might settle down in a riverbank, hollow tree, or log. Nesting inside a tree would give you protection from predators and the elements, such as rain, snow, and wind. Or you might make your den inside a barn or a shed. When you got hungry, you might eat crayfish or frogs living in a brook, steal eggs from birds' nests, or dine on fruit and plants.

If you were a city or town raccoon, you might have to find shelter in the attic or basement of a human home. That sounds like a good deal, but most humans don't enjoy having raccoons as roommates, so you might be kicked out if you're found. Your city dinner might come from a garbage can or a food dish left outside for someone's pet.

RIDGESIDE CAVERN

Carved by flowing water into a rocky outcrop, this cavern becomes a cool place to retreat and relax. Whether you want to chill in your cave or venture outside for a little sun, this den offers the best of both! There are three indoor levels to design and decorate, and scenic outdoor space as well.

LIGHT IT UP
Is your den too dark? Illuminate this underground space with lamps and holiday lights!

A STURDY SETTING
The furniture items made for this cool cavern are all carved from stone.

GAME: Play Wild
DEN TYPE: Land
COST: 150 Sapphire
SPECIAL WALLS AND FLOORS?: No
INSIDER INFO: Looking for the best views in this rocky, roomy den? Cross the log near the top to walk out on your own private patio and take in all the breathtaking scenery!

ALL ABOUT THE CLIMB

To get to the different levels of this den, you'll need to climb a few sets of stone steps. Feeling winded? One of the most famous staircases in the world is Chand Baori in India. It's a well that's 100 feet (30 m) deep and covered in 3,500 intricate stone steps.

CARVED BY WATER

The smooth walls and floor of this den are a welcome sight to all who might call this cozy cave home. Underground caverns in nature are often created when running water wears down rock over time.

Crazy Cool Caves

 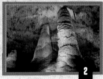 

1   **2**   **3**

You can go to an art museum to see a work of breathtaking beauty—or you can visit a cavern or a cave. Some of them are home to incredible colors and amazing rock formations. Here's a quick tour of some of the most amazing caves in the world:

1. **The Blue Grotto, Italy:** Light illuminating this cave gives it a brilliant blue glow.
2. **Carlsbad Caverns, New Mexico, U.S.A.:** The many chambers of these caverns are filled with unusual rock formations. One of the most famous is the White Giant, a chamber that contains a huge white stalagmite.
3. **Marble Caves, Patagonia, Chile:** The beautiful, swirled marble formations in these caves were created by lake currents over a period of 6,000 years. The color changes throughout the year, depending on the light.

ALPINE LODGE

Are you the outdoorsy type who loves hiking and camping? Then this mountaintop den is the perfect home for you. Hang out in this rustic lodge and enjoy the fresh air and spectacular views.

TOUGH TREES

Choose this beautiful den, and you'll be surrounded by coniferous trees—including evergreen trees like these, that produce cones. Coniferous trees can survive the cold, high winds and lack of moisture on tall mountain peaks.

PICNIC PEAK

This flat ledge with a great view would be a great place to create a patio or picnic area.

HIGH ALTITUDE

What animals will you see way up high on Jamaa's peaks? In the wild, mountain dwellers living at between 8,000 and 12,000 feet (2,438 and 3,659 m) above sea level are living in high altitude. There, the oxygen levels are lower, and so is air pressure.

AJ Stats

GAME: Play Wild
DEN TYPE: Land
COST: 150 Sapphires
SPECIAL WALLS AND FLOORS?: No
INSIDER INFO: This den is perfect for Jammers who love wide-open spaces. With tall ceilings inside and lots of outdoor space to decorate, you can try out tons of different styles and themes.

FRESH-AIR DESIGN

Decorate the outdoor area of your den with stone pathways, bubbling ponds, and rustic chairs that invite your visitors to chill out and enjoy the beauty of nature.

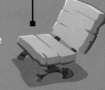

CLIFF HOTEL

If you want your next vacation to be a real cliff-hanger, check out the Aescher Mountain Guesthouse in Switzerland. The 170-year-old inn and restaurant is built against a cliff face in the Swiss Alps almost 4,800 feet (1,463 m) above sea level. Visitors can climb up the peak to get to the inn. Or, if an extreme mountain trek isn't your thing, you can catch a cable car to the top instead. Once there, guests walk along a footpath that takes them through a prehistoric cave straight to the hotel's doorstep. When visitors aren't hanging out in the hotel's rustic dorm rooms, they can hike around the lodge or dine at the restaurant perched on the edge of the bluff. But no matter what activities you do, one thing's for sure: At this mountainside inn you'll always have a rockin' view.

IN THE RED

Build on the striking color outside this den and decorate with red walls, red rugs, and red furniture.

THE ALPHAS' DENS

IF YOU'VE BEEN EXPLORING JAMAA, THEN YOU PROBABLY HAVE MET SOME OF THE ALPHAS—and encountered the dark Phantoms, too! Their stories are linked to the history of Jamaa.

LONG AGO, THE ANIMALS OF JAMAA LIVED PEACEFULLY, WATCHED OVER BY MIRA AND ZIOS, JAMAA'S GUARDIAN SPIRITS. After a time, the animals of Jamaa began to distrust one another and refused to work together. During this dark period, mysterious portals opened, and the rotten Phantoms came, destroying the land and polluting the waters.

Mira and **Zios** needed champions to defeat the Phantoms. They named six leaders: **Liza**, the panda; **Graham**, the monkey; **Cosmo**, the koala; **Peck**, the bunny; **Sir Gilbert**, the tiger; and **Greely**, the wolf. Working together, they drove the Phantoms from the land and restored Jamaa.

Each of the Alphas has his or her own den in Animal Jam—and now Jammers can own dens just like theirs!

COSMO'S TREE HOUSE

GAME: Animal Jam
DEN TYPE: Land
COST: 7 Diamonds
SPECIAL WALLS AND FLOORS?: Yes. Most wallpapers are nature themed, while the floors appear as rugs scattered throughout the den.
INSIDER INFO: This den is the perfect place to bring the outdoors in. Decorate this den with plants, water features, and items made from natural materials such as wood and stone.

LIZA'S GARDEN

GAME: Animal Jam
DEN TYPE: Land
COST: 7 Diamonds
SPECIAL WALLS AND FLOORS?: Yes. Some styles have bamboo patterns; others feature traditional symbols from Chinese culture.

INSIDER INFO: This peaceful den is where the adventurous panda Alpha rests from her travels. The serene gardens around the den are ideal for wandering and relaxing.

PECK'S DEN

GAME: Animal Jam
DEN TYPE: Land
COST: 7 Diamonds
SPECIAL WALLS AND FLOORS?: Yes. Many styles, such as the Planet Walls, get a splattered-paint look.
INSIDER INFO: Like other bunnies, Peck is most comfortable in an underground home with many different rooms. As an artist, it's not a coincidence that part of Peck's Den is inside a giant geode filled with jewels of every color. Try walking on one of the trampolines inside and see what happens!

GREELY'S HIDEOUT

GAME: Animal Jam
DEN TYPE: Land
COST: 7 Diamonds
SPECIAL WALLS AND FLOORS?: Yes. The Yellow Sweets and Bat Wallpaper become Phantoms.
INSIDER INFO: If you like the Volcano, Greely's Hideout takes it to another level—levels, actually. This multi-layered den has bridges that take you over pools of bubbling lava to different areas of the hideout. What kind of secrets is the wolf Alpha hiding inside his shadowy den?

GAME: Animal Jam
DEN TYPE: Land
COST: 7 Diamonds
SPECIAL WALLS AND FLOORS?:
Yes. Some patterns look like stained glass, the perfect fit for a medieval castle.
INSIDER INFO: The tiger Alpha's den is one of the most majestic dens in Jamaa. With its red and gold decorations, stained-glass windows, towers, and water features, it's a palace fit for the most regal Jammers in Jamaa.

GRAHAM'S OBSERVATORY

GAME: Animal Jam
DEN TYPE: Land
COST: 7 Diamonds
SPECIAL WALLS AND FLOORS?: Yes. You'll see lots of gears, just like the gears always turning in Graham's head.
INSIDER INFO: The inquisitive monkey Alpha's den is perfect for Jammers who love to tinker and invent! There is plenty of space in Graham's Observatory to store all your gear, gadgets, and gizmos.

DECK OUT YOUR DEN!

What's the best thing about decorating your den? There are no rules! Do you want to add ice sculptures to a Volcano? No problem! Fill a Beach House with candy? Go ahead! Or maybe you just want to make a nice, comfy den where you and your buddies can chill. That's cool, too! Not sure how to start? Don't worry. In this section, you'll learn tips and tricks for decking out your den in style.

SHOP AND STYLE FROM YOUR DEN

YOU DON'T NEED TO LEAVE YOUR DEN TO BEGIN STYLING IT WITH THE LATEST AND GREATEST DEN ITEMS. Start by clicking the **Edit Den button** . Then follow these steps:

SHOP:

Click the **Shop for Your Den button**. In Animal Jam, this is a direct link to Jam Mart Furniture, where you'll find many different den items. In Play Wild, you'll have your choice between three different shops: Jam Mart Furniture, the Sapphire Shop, and Claws 'N Paws.

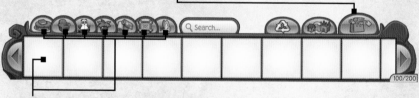

100/200

STORE YOUR STUFF:

After you purchase an item, it will appear in one of the slots in the bar at the bottom of your screen. Buttons on top of the bar help organize your items so that you can find them quickly.

TO FIND OUT MORE ABOUT PETS AND PET ACCESSORIES, GO TO PAGE 70.

 All your items in one place!

 Furniture of all shapes and sizes

 Decorations, including plushies

 Potted plants, flowers, trees, bushes, and more

 Wallpaper and flooring

 Wall decorations, windows, and Masterpieces

 All your pets can hang out in your den!

How to Get More Stuff

Sure, you can shop from your den, but that's not the only place to shop on Jamaa. In fact, it's not even the only way to get your favorite den items!

HIT THE SHOPS

You may have already found some cool den items in Jam Mart Furniture, but there are shops all over Jamaa that sell things you can't find here (see page 66 for a full list of shops)!

GO TO PARTIES

Parties sell exclusive items and accessories you can't get anywhere else. Each party has its own shop, so keep your eyes on your Party List to see when all the cool parties are happening.

COMPLETE THE JOURNEY BOOK

When you explore the lands and oceans of Jamaa, you may come across plants and animals that live there. You can click them to fill the empty slots in your **Journey Book** . Each time you fill a page in your book, you will earn an exclusive den item that can't be found anywhere else!

Decorating Tips

PLAN:

If you have a large den, move to the area you want to decorate before clicking the **Edit Den button** . Then your items will pop up close to where you want them.

ROTATE:

When you're placing an item in your den, you can click the **arrow** to rotate the item so it will face in a different direction.

RECYCLE:

If you're not using an item and want to get rid of it, there are two things you can do: You can either trade it with another Jammer (see page 65) or recycle it. When you recycle an item, you will earn some Gems for it, but not as many as you paid to buy the item in the first place. Click the **Edit Den button** and then the **Recycle Items button** . Then click an item, and you'll see how many Gems you'll get in return.

VISIT:

Need some decorating inspiration? Visit the dens of other Jammers. (See page 10 for a how-to.) It's OK to let ideas from other Jammers inspire your own!

IF YOU'RE VISITING ANOTHER JAMMER'S DEN, BE POLITE! SAY HELLO AND GIVE A COMPLIMENT IF YOU LIKE THE DEN.

TRY A THEME:

Items in the shops often relate to different themes, so you can create a unique environment in your den when you put these items together. For example, a Dig Site Canopy, Pottery Shards, and a Buried Statue can turn your den into an archaeological dig!

Trading Tips

TRADING IS A SUPERFUN WAY TO DECK OUT YOUR DEN. There are many ways to do it. You may have noticed as you walk around Jamaa the bubbles above animals saying things like, "Trade with me plz." This means just what it says—that Jammers want to trade! You may also notice the **Trade icon** 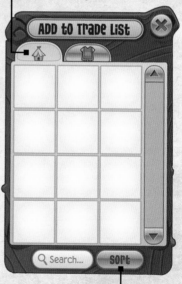 floating next to your buddies. This means they are in the middle of a trade!

BEFORE YOU CAN TRADE, YOU HAVE TO HAVE SOMETHING TO TRADE FOR. Go to your **animal customization menu** and click the **Trade tab** at the top. Then click the **plus button**. It will take you to your items so you can look through and decide what you are ready to let go of. Once you decide, just click it and it will be added to your **Trade List!**

TRADE LIST:
You can put accessories and den items on your **Trade List**.

ADD tO TrAde LiSt

Q Search...   SOrt

Wanna Trade?

SORT:
Use the Sort and Search options to quickly find that special item that you're looking for.

When someone asks if anyone wants to trade, click their name tag to bring up their Player Card. Click the **Trade tab** and their **Trade List** will pop up. You can scroll through it and see if there's anything you'd like to trade for. If there is, click it, then click the **plus button** ⊕ and add what you would like to trade for.

REMEMBER, JAMMERS:

Trading is permanent, so only trade items you are sure you want to get rid of. Sometimes people may say things like "trust trade" or "let me try it on," or they may want you to trade them through Jam-A-Grams. If you see one of these Jammers, it's not a good idea to trade with them. The Trading System exists to keep all trades fair, and smart Jammers always use it!

TRADE WITH ANY PLAYER:

The Trading System is a safe and fair way to trade with other Jammers, even if they're not your buddies. This is where you'll see who you're trading with.

YOUR ITEM:

This is where you'll see the item you're trading.

TRADE REQUESTED

New Jammer wants to trade their **4** items

Precious Snowflake

4 items

for your

Do you want to trade?

TRADE ✓ ✗ CANCEL

WHAT YOU'LL GET:

Jammers can offer up to 20 items to trade.

ACCEPT OR CANCEL:

Ready to accept or walk away? Click these buttons to end the trading session.

let's talk SHOP

YOU WILL FIND SHOPS SELLING UNIQUE DEN ITEMS IN EVERY CORNER OF JAMAA. Check back with them often, because new items pop up all the time.

ADVENTURE SHOP

Fascinated with Phantoms? Pick up a Phantom Cell or a Phantom Coop at this shop in Adventure Base Camp.

CLAWS 'N PAWS

Head inside the giant tree in Appondale and go upstairs to find items for your pet.

ROYAL RIDGE

Fly up to this cliffside shop in Coral Canyons to find some of the fanciest den items in Jamaa.

DIAMOND SHOP

This shop in Jamaa Township sells animals, dens, items, pets, accessories, and more! Remember: You can only use Diamonds to purchase things in this shop.

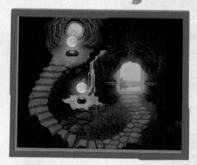

FLAG SHOP

You'll find everything in this Sarepia Forest shop, from a Pirate Flag, to a Peace Flag, to the flag of your favorite country.

EPIC WONDERS

Hidden behind the waterfall in Coral Canyons, this shop offers rare mystical items.

JAM MART FURNITURE

You can buy the basics for your den here at this essential Jamaa Township shop. Plus, you can access it directly from your den.

SUNKEN TREASURES
You can buy nautical items in this underwater shop in Kani Cove. There's also a shop within a shop here: the Ocean Diamond Shop, where you can buy some of the coolest ocean items in Jamaa.

MARINE MARVELS
Dive down down down to this shop in Deep Blue to purchase stone statues for your underwater den.

OUTBACK IMPORTS
Fill your den with rustic furnishings and decorations from this shop in Kimbara Outback.

SOL ARCADE SHOP
Buy arcade machines here at this Jamaa Township shop, so you can play your favorite games right from your den!

STUDIO CORNER

Artistic Jammers shop at this Coral Canyons outlet for paint supplies and easels to make Masterpieces!

TOPIARY SHOP

Stop at this shop in Sarepia Forest to find amazing hedges sculpted to look like animals.

TREETOP GARDENS

Build your own garden with indoor and outdoor plants found at this Sarepia Forest shop.

ONLY IN PLAY WILD!

YOU CAN FIND MANY OF THE SHOPS FROM ANIMAL JAM IN PLAY WILD. YOU WON'T FIND THE DIAMOND SHOP THERE, THOUGH. IN PLAY WILD, THE SAPPHIRE SHOP IS THE PLACE TO GO FOR THE BEST ANIMALS, ITEMS, PETS, DENS, AND MORE.

ANCIENT ANTIQUITIES

If fossils are more your style, stop by this shop in Balloosh to pick up a piece of ancient history.

TURN YOUR DEN INTO ...
a Pet Paradise!

WOULDN'T IT BE GREAT TO COME HOME TO YOUR DEN and find all your pets happily waiting for you? It's easy to make that happen! All it takes is three steps:

100/200

1. Click the **Edit Den button** 🔘.

2. Click the **Pets button.**

3. Click the pet you want to move into your den. Drag it to where you want it, and then drop it there.

INSIDER INFO

Your pet will hang out in that part of the den as long as you leave it there. It won't move or perform actions unless you click it. To make your pet feel right at home, you can purchase pet beds, bowls, toys, and playhouses for your den. Look for these items in the Pet Den Item Shop on the second floor of Claws 'N Paws in Appondale.

1 Mister Wonkybuddy

PLACING ONE PET IN YOUR DEN IS NICE. But adding a bunch of fluffy, feathery, creepy-crawly, cuddly, and cute pets to your den and loading it with pet accessories can turn your pad into a pet palace! There are so many awesome items your pet will love. Check out this amazing pet paradise.

TEENY DOOR:
If you've got a mouse in your house, it'll appreciate this Mouse Door that is just its size.

TINY HOMES:
Fill your den with mini dens for your pet, such as this Pet Cardboard Castle.

THE WILD HISTORY OF HAMSTERS

Adorable hamsters are popular pets in Jamaa. Players have fun dressing them up in hats and watching them play on tiny castles. What players might not know is that these cute critters have a wild history!

Before 1930, hamsters were not kept as pets. That's the year zoologist Israel Aharoni captured 12 Syrian, or golden hamsters, in the Middle East. Aharoni brought them back to Jerusalem, and their children were given to zoos and universities around the world.

In 1971, more hamsters were captured and brought to the United States. Today, the golden hamster is the most popular pet hamster in North America. If you see a golden hamster spinning in a wheel, it is probably a descendant of those hamsters caught by Aharoni almost 90 years ago!

TURN YOUR DEN INTO ...
a Masterpiece Museum!

PLAIN WALLS CAN BE BORING, RIGHT? Luckily, there are many different ways to decorate the walls of your den. You can change the wallpaper and add stained-glass windows and colorful wall hangings. But Jammers who truly love to customize their dens fill them with Masterpieces that they create or that are made by other Jammers.

hat's a Masterpiece? It's a work of original art you can make, frame, and hang in your den. Here's how to make your own Masterpiece:

Art Studio

1. Visit the Art Studio in Coral Canyons.

2. Click the **easel** featuring a painting of Peck.

3. Choose between the Painting and Pixel Painting activities.

4. Use the tools to make a work of art.

5. When you're happy with your painting, click the **Create Den Item button** (create den item) and choose your favorite frame. It will cost you two Diamonds to create your Masterpiece.

6. Animal Jam will review your Masterpiece to make sure it follows the guidelines. It may take up to a week, so be patient! When it's approved, you can hang your Masterpiece in your den and trade it with others. Your username will appear in the frame.

CREATIVE SPACE:
Turn any den into an artist's retreat! Look for items in the Paint Studio collection or other artsy items. Decorate your den with colorful Paint Splats as well as tools such as a Paint Mixer, Paint Roller, and more.

INSIDER INFO

Buy a Pixel Easel from the Studio Shop and put it in your den. With this easel, you can make pixelated Masterpieces by carefully coloring in one square at a time.

HANG OUT WITH BUDDIES!

Hey Buddy!

AFTER YOU'VE DECORATED YOUR DEN, YOU MIGHT WANT TO SHOW IT OFF. You can always invite your buddies to come visit you. If they accept your invitation, make them feel welcome! Use the chat bar to greet them when they come to your den.

WHEN YOUR BUDDIES COME OVER, INVITE THEM TO DANCE OR PLAY. It helps if you have some den items that your guests can interact with. Some items, such as the arcade games or the Smoothie Machine, open up games or activities you can play. Other items do fun things when you click them.

The Epic Train Set will run on the track when you click it, and you can bake a cake when you click the items in the Cake Bake Kitchen. Lots of den items have clickable secrets, so when you add new ones to your den, experiment and see what happens!

Epic Train Set

CONNECT WITH PORTALS

Want to get to your best buddy's den in a hurry? Install a portal in your den! When you place the portal in your den, a **Buddies icon** will come up. Click it to choose one buddy from your list. When you're playing in your den, the portal will glow when you approach it. Jump in, and you'll instantly transport to your buddy's den! You can even have more than one portal to connect with multiple buddies.

How to Invite Your Buddies Over:

1. First, make sure your den is unlocked by clicking the **My Settings icon** ⚙ in the upper right of your screen.

2. Then check to see which of your buddies are online by clicking the **Buddies icon** 🐾 on the top left of your screen. A list of your buddies will appear, and any buddy with a green dot next to his or her name is online.

3. Click the buddy's name to bring up their Player Card. Click the **Send a Jam-A-Gram button** 📧 to send a Jam-A-Gram.

4. Choose the card you want to send. Then click the **plus button** ➕ to choose a message. Select "Let's be buddies," and then click "Come to my den!"

5. Click the **Send button** 📧 to send your message to your buddy.

Insider Info

Entertain your visiting buddies by mixing up the music when they visit your den! Play your favorite tunes. Or play music that will get everyone dancing, like "Sky High" or "Jam On." Or take requests—ask your buddies what kind of music they'd like to hear and play it for them.

LET'S JAM!

EPIC DENS

The best way to get inspiration for your den is by checking out the Epic Dens. Some Epic Dens are created by Animal Jam HQ and feature rare never-before-seen den items. Others are Epic Dens created by Jammers just like you! In this section, you'll see some of the coolest Epic Dens ever created by AJHQ.

What Makes A Den Epic?

AN EPIC DEN IS A DEN THAT'S CLEARLY BEEN GIVEN A LOT OF LOVE BY ITS OWNER, AND HAS BEEN CUSTOMIZED IN A CREATIVE WAY. It could be a huge Crystal Palace or a Small House. The size of the den doesn't matter—it's what you put into it.

A JHQ selects only the most Epic Dens in Jamaa to be on the list, so Jammers can get pretty competitive when trying to get noticed. Follow these tips to create a memorable epic den.

DISCOVER EPIC DENS: To check out the newest Epic Dens, go to the World Map and click the **Epic Dens button** . Here you'll see a list of the latest Epic Dens.

WORLD MAP

Epic Dens

Pixel Place

Bouncing Sillystone
Gorgeous Redplum
Rosy Stronglady
Empress Jazzyfeet
Hopefull Glassivy
Swaggy Coolmaster
Old Happyleopard
Sneaky Laughingdoll
Fabulous Sillypanda
Flora Prettyspike

INSIDER INFO

Enter a den contest! Be sure to read the **Daily Explorer,** Animal Jam's official blog, frequently. Sometimes there are den contests with a prize for the winner.

TOP TIPS ON HOW to Make it onto the EPic Dens List

1. PLAY OFTEN!

The more you play, the more stuff you'll be able to get, since certain items are available on different days and during different seasons. Plus, the more you log in, the more ideas and creativity will come your way!

2. UNLOCK YOUR DEN AND SPREAD THE WORD

Your den is awesome and you'll want to be able to show it off—especially once you make the list! Host den parties and invite all of your buddies to see how cool it is. The more Jammers that check out your den, the more chances you'll have to get noticed.

3. MAKE THE BEST USE OF YOUR SPACE

Your den doesn't necessarily have to be overflowing with items, but make sure your space isn't empty.

INSIDER INFO

When you explore an official AJHQ Epic Den, click on everything you see! You might find secret items for sale.

4. GET CREATIVE

Sure, you could place a couch in the living space, but what if it was on the porch surrounded by Tiki Torches? Think outside the box when it comes to decorating your space. Consider picking a theme for your den (see page 63 for more ideas). Or use items that match to create a look that makes a statement—all rustic, all colorful, all plants— there are so many options! Another fun way to decorate is to make something that isn't available in the game by using what you have. For example, you can make a dance floor using expertly placed lights. You can make new rooms, or even a maze or labyrinth, out of shoji screens, fences, or other items that could serve as dividers.

Crystal Palace

The Crystal Palace is one of the biggest dens in Jamaa, with lots of rooms and levels to explore. The crystal statues of the six Alphas make it a favorite of Jammers everywhere. It's not often found in the Diamond Shop, so when you see it, grab it—and make it even more epic when you customize it!

AWESOME ALPHAS

You can't have too many Alpha statues!

A BEAUTIFUL VIEW

Enjoy the spectacular view from the lookout tower.

SPARKLING FLOORS

In this den, the Flower Carpet turns into pink crystals.

AN OCEAN OF FUN

Water-loving Jammers will love being so close to the ocean.

FLOWER POWER

Adding more plants and flowers brings color to this den.

CRYSTAL MINE

Descend underground into the glittering crystal mine.

FUN FUNGUS

Mounds of mushrooms give the mine a fantasy feel.

AJ stats

GAME: Animal Jam
DECORATED BY: AJHQ
DEN TYPE: Land
COST: 7 Diamonds
SPECIAL WALLS AND FLOORS?: Yes. The existing shapes transform into glittering jewels and crystals.

INSIDER INFO

This den takes the crystal theme and builds on it, choosing items and even plants in pretty crystal colors. You can make your den epic by picking a color theme—bold colors, bright colors, black and white—and making a statement.

COOL CRYSTALS

A grain of salt is an example of a crystal. So is a snowflake. And even a ruby. How can three very different things all be crystals? It's all about how crystals form. When minerals are in liquid form and then cool very slowly, they become solid. The atoms in the minerals bond, forming molecules, and then those molecules bond and form shapes.

Different molecules make different types of crystals. Take that grain of salt. Salt crystals form when sodium and chlorine atoms bond together. Salt crystals are shaped like a perfect cube, and every salt molecule is the same exact shape.

81

EPIC HAUNTED MANOR

This den is similar to the Haunted House, but bigger and creepier. Don't be surprised to find Phantoms hanging around this den—they love it! And so do Jammers who are not afraid to take a walk on the scary side. If you have a chance to visit this den, be sure to click around for some spooky surprises!

CREEPY CELLAR

The basement is the perfect place to build a mad scientist's lab!

AJ STATS

GAME: Animal Jam
DECORATED BY: AJHQ
DEN TYPE: Land
COST: 5 Diamonds
SPECIAL WALLS AND FLOORS?: Yes.
The styles take on the spooky,
peeling look of a dusty
haunted house.

BAD MOON RISING

A full moon casts an eerie glow
over the den.

HAUNTED FOREST

Wait—do these trees
have faces?

SQUASH GARDEN

Plant your own pumpkin patch.

SPOOKY DECOR

Old-timey furniture sets the right
mood for scares.

WILD WALLS

Comes with fun Phantom wallpaper.

INSIDER INFO

The designer of this
den paid as much
attention to the
outside of the den
as the inside, creat-
ing both a grave-
yard and a pumpkin
patch. Make sure to
decorate every inch
of your den to make
it epic, too!

GHOSTLY GRAVEYARD

Adding a few dozen
tombstones can turn
your backyard into a
spooky cemetery.

POISON POND

Swim in this toxic
swamp—if you
dare—to get a
spooky surprise.

JAMAALIDAY HOUSE

When the Jamaaliday season rolls around, it's nice to invite buddies over to celebrate. This giant gingerbread house is perfect for a holiday party. You can load it with candy-themed den items and accessories.

WARM UP

Sing some Jamaaliday songs around a candy campfire—while sitting on a marsh-mallow seat.

CHOCOLATE DIP

Yes, that's a swimming pool, and yes, it's filled with chocolate! Take a dip to see what happens!

AJ stats

GAME: Animal Jam
DECORATED BY: AJHQ
DEN TYPE: Land
COST: 5 Diamonds
SPECIAL WALLS AND FLOORS?: Yes. Everything looks like candy!

FABULOUS FEAST
It wouldn't be the Jamaaliday season without lots of tasty treats to eat. Include some to make your den a festive place to be.

FA-LA-LA-LA PHANTOM
Even Phantoms get in the Jamaaliday spirit!

HOLIDAY LIGHTS
Lots of lights add warmth and glow.

INSIDER INFO

When it's time to decorate for the Jamaalidays, think: more, more, more! More candy, more color, more lights. This den is overflowing with holiday cheer, which is what makes it epic!

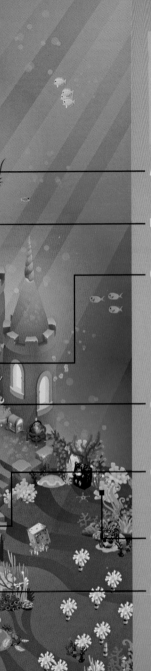

If you're living under the sea, you might as well do it in style! The Sandcastle is the most majestic underwater den in Jamaa, with lots of towers and levels. You don't have to be a prince or a princess to enjoy this royal retreat, either. It's a great home for any of Jamaa's ocean animals.

A GOOD DEFENSE

Cannons on the turrets are to scare off marauding pirates.

PIRATE'S BOOTY

Nothing sparkles like a glittering pile of treasure!

CRAZY FOR KELP

You won't be able to get enough kelp in this den! Sea kelp is one of the fastest growing organisms on the planet. Large forests of it grow at the bottom of the ocean. Sea urchins love to eat kelp—and it's a nutritious food for humans to eat, too!

CAPTAIN'S QUARTERS

Every sea captain needs a place to write down a log of their adventures.

CASTLE GUARDIAN

This Dolphin Venus Statue diligently watches over the Sandcastle.

COLORFUL PLANTS

Using lots of ocean plants adds epic color to this den.

DECK OUT EACH LEVEL

Add furniture to this patio to make it a great space to hang out.

AJ stats

GAME: Animal Jam
DECORATED BY: AJHQ
DEN TYPE: Ocean
COST: 7 Diamonds
SPECIAL WALLS AND
FLOORS?: No

INSIDER INFO

This epic den does something different with each level— something you can do in your own den. Make one level a game room, one level an indoor garden—whatever you do is up to you!

DIG DEEPER INTO DENS

BY THIS TIME, YOU MIGHT HAVE SPENT HOURS DECORATING YOUR DENS IN ANIMAL JAM AND PLAY WILD. Why not? It's fun! But don't forget that you have a den outside the world of Jamaa, too. Here are some ideas for having fun with dens at home or in your community:

1

HOST A MASTERPIECE PARTY WITH YOUR FRIENDS! Ask everyone to create one or more pieces of art. Get together and trade with each other. Then hang up your Masterpieces in your home.

LET ANIMAL JAM INSPIRE YOU TO DECORATE YOUR OWN ROOM. Hang up pictures of your favorite animals. Or take it a step further and decorate your room to match your favorite den—if you love the Tiger Temple, for example, add red and orange pillows, blankets, and curtains to give your room a rain forest look.

2

3

DOES YOUR TOWN HAVE AN ANIMAL SHELTER? With the help of a parent, contact them and see if the animals there need gently used blankets, towels, or other things to make their temporary dens comfy. Ask friends and family if they have any items they can donate.

FIND OUT HOW YOUR FAVORITE ANIMAL MAKES ITS DEN, AND MAKE A DIORAMA OF WHAT IT LOOKS LIKE. Bring the diorama to school to share with your classmates, or use it to decorate your room.

4

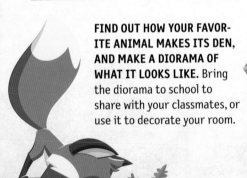

FINAL WORDS FROM

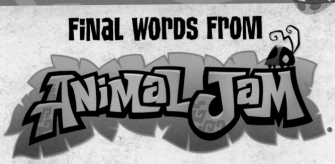

ANIMAL JAM

WE'RE SO GLAD THAT YOU'VE CHOSEN TO ENTER THE **WORLD OF ANIMAL JAM!** It's so cool to see kids who love animals and their homes as much as you do.

There are a few final things to remember as your journey continues. First, all dens are awesome! It doesn't matter if it's superbly small or fabulously fancy. As long as you love it, that's what matters. Also, don't forget to have fun! Remember, there are no rules for how you should design your den. Take your time and experiment until you find the home that's perfect for you. There's no right or wrong way to do it. And finally, keep logging in! Animal Jam is always changing. There will always be new dens to explore, new items in the shops, and new parties with special items you can get for your awesome animal abode.

Now that you know everything you need to know about Animal Jam's dens, it's time to jump in feetfirst. There's a whole world of adventures waiting for you in Jamaa. Get out there and play wild!

—*Animal Jam*

INDEX

Boldface indicates illustrations.

INDEX

CREDITS

Published in conjunction with WildWorks, Inc. Animal Jam is a trademark of WildWorks, Inc., used under license. All rights reserved.

Published by National Geographic Partners, LLC. All rights reserved. Reproduction of the whole or any part of the contents without written permission from the publisher is prohibited.

Since 1888, the National Geographic Society has funded more than 12,000 research, exploration, and preservation projects around the world. The Society receives funds from National Geographic Partners, LLC, funded in part by your purchase. A portion of the proceeds from this book supports this vital work. To learn more, visit natgeo.com/info.

NATIONAL GEOGRAPHIC and Yellow Border Design are trademarks of the National Geographic Society, used under license.

For more information, visit nationalgeographic.com, call 1-800-647-5463, or write to the following address:

National Geographic Partners
1145 17th Street N.W.
Washington, D.C. 20036-4688 U.S.A.

Visit us online at:
nationalgeographic.com/books

For librarians and teachers:
ngchildrensbooks.org

More for kids from National Geographic:
natgeokids.com

For information about special discounts for bulk purchases, please contact National Geographic Books Special Sales: specialsales@natgeo.com

For rights or permissions inquiries, please contact National Geographic Books Subsidiary Rights: bookrights@natgeo.com

Designed by Stephanie White

The publisher would like to thank the following people for making this book possible: Kate Hale, executive editor; Callie Broaddus, senior designer; Sarah J. Mock, senior photo editor; Alix Inchausti, production editor; and Anne LeongSon and Gus Tello, production assistants. Special thanks also to all the creative and production teams at WildWorks, Inc.

Hardcover ISBN: 978-1-4263-3146-6
Reinforced library binding ISBN:
978-1-4263-3147-3

Printed in China
18/RRDH/1

PLAY WILD!

Have fun with 100 Jamaa-inspired challenges, including word puzzles, quizzes, trivia, and more.

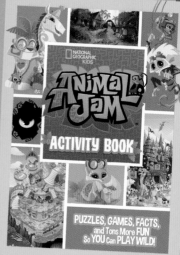

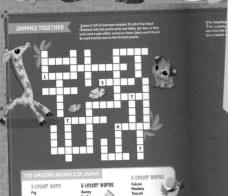